Dadtastic!

With love to devoted dads everywhere

Martha Valentine

PORTICO

With special thanks to Malcolm Croft, Jack Noel, Katie Cowan, Zoe Anspach and all at Anova Books

First published in the United Kingdom in 2010 by
Portico Books
10 Southcombe Street
London
W14 0RA

An imprint of Anova Books Company Ltd

Cover and inside illustrations by Jack Noel (www.jacknoel.co.uk)

ISBN 9781906032821

A CIP catalogue record for this book is available from the British Library.

10 9 8 7 6 5 4 3 2 1

Printed and bound by J.P.Printers SDN. BHD., Malaysia

This book can be ordered direct from the publisher at www.anovabooks.com

For Dad

Introduction

Dads. What would we do without them? They may get the raw deal next to mums, and nowhere near as much of the credit or attention, but they are always there for you when you need them. Or more commonly, when you need their wallet. Or car. Or advice. Or for them to buy you beer from the local shop. And for those many reasons alone they should all be celebrated – each and every kind. Having spent most of their adult life looking after their kids, losing their hair and gaining a belly, and being labelled 'gross' (when all they want is a kiss from mum), you would think that dads deserve a quiet life where they can indulge their passions – beer, cars, barbecues and mum. But, oh no, being a dad means being around 24hrs a day, 7 days a

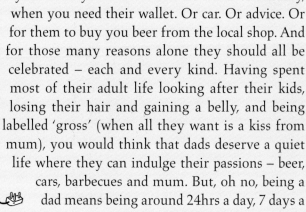

week at everyone's beck and call *and* letting the kids walk in and out of *your* house as freely as they please. Essentially, then, dads are like fancy hotels. They never close, have loyal staff and people constantly take things they presume are free.

So, next time you spot your tired, hungry (mum's put him on a diet again), unshaven, skint and, no doubt, grumpy dad, don't give him grief and call him names, no matter how irresistible it may be. No, go up to him, give him a kiss and a hug and tell him you love him. He'll be cynical at first, thinking you want something, but once he sees you genuinely mean it, watch as his eyes glow with appreciation and unconditional, uncontrollable, love. Dads always sleep better when they know they are loved.

Like dogs.

Dads. *What would we do without them?*

Teacher Dad

Dads, for all young boys and girls, are role models. Someone to look up to and learn from. So, OK, dads don't know everything there is to know in the world but they sure know a lot, and this type of dad likes to impart his life lessons and experiences on to all his children, and, well, to anyone else who will listen.

Teacher dad is a knowledgeable dad and, by god, he knows it, so when his children come to him needing advice, this dad is in his element. He gets his books out, draws maps, scribbles notes, scratches his beard, anything he can, to be as much help to his

children who are calling out for his help. Deep down inside this type of dad, he is incredibly chuffed that his children see him as a fountain of knowledge, a wise man, a genius, if you will!

Whether it's a forthcoming maths test, how to parallel park or even how to charm a woman (because he didn't do too badly, apparently), teacher dad likes to constantly tell his children all the life lessons he's learned and how it made him 'a richer person'. Not literally rich, he'll add. He'll blame mum for that.

Have you seen this Dad?

Teacher dads are great. They know loads. Of course, as the children get older, and smarter, teacher dad starts worrying that they won't need him any more – but they do. Kids always make mistakes, and teacher dad will always be on hand to teach them a lesson!

Gadget Dad

Dads are renowned for being suckers. Not only will they let the kids get away with murder (as long as mum doesn't find out!), dads can also be bought and sold if it means a chance to have an easy life. Well, dads are also suckers for anything new, shiny, electronic (with strength measured in horsepower!) and advertised on telly as the coolest, shiniest and most must-have machine on the market. Whether it's a new 100-blade razor, a new DVD player, stereo (with surround sound!), 5megapixel phone or home multimedia network system, dads can't resist them. They want it all, they want it now and they'll trample over the in-laws to get one today. Especially if it has uniquely formulated dad-words like 'mach' or 'ultra' in the title!

All across the country, right now, dads are browsing Amazon or wandering through a home electronics shop with their wallet burning a hole in their pocket, wondering what new and exciting piece of tat they can fill the living room with. Mum looks on disapprovingly, worried about where on earth they are going to put it all. Of course, these types of dad aren't shy about buying these gadgets, oh no. Once they are home, unboxed, set up and turned up to 11, this type of dad invites the neighbours around to proudly show off his elegant bit of equipment.

Car-mad Dad

All dads are car mad. Whether they want to be or not, and whether they know it or not, it's part of a dad's duty in life to be able to fix the car (without using a manual!) from the smallest of problems such as changing a tyre right through to observing that 'the exhaust has gone' from merely wafting the engine. This car wisdom is part of a dad's DNA

(Dad's 'Nowledge of Automobiles) and helps him understand the difference between a camshaft and a supercharger and a torque converter and a windscreen wiper without needing to phone a friend. Other, normal, people have no idea how a catalytic converter works, and quite frankly, aren't fussed to find out anytime soon. But not car-mad dads – they know all the latest models, brands and types of car there is (since the first one ever!) and can be found quite frequently with their head underneath the bonnet, overalls covered in oil (how is mum going to get that out?) muttering car-lingo to themselves, trying to sound like a professional mechanic. Car-mad dad, we love you, but come in from the garage will you, your dinner's getting cold…

Survival Weekend Dad

Dad's are discipline crazy. They like order, organisation and a clear-cut route from how to get from A to B. They don't like any funny business or foolish shenanigans, and they certainly don't like mum mucking about with his timetable just because she needs to change her dress for the umpteenth time. If this type of dad says he wants to be out the house by 6.02am (to get to the airport precisely two hours ahead of the schedule) then, by golly, he will be out of the house dot on 6.02am, and not a minute later, even if the cat is staring at an empty bowl wondering where the hell you are all going with those massive, well-packed bags!

A survival weekend dad likes to experience nature first-hand with his children, going on trains to the countryside, pitching tents, going for long, long, *long* walks, getting muddy and even running around assault courses, eating paraffin-infused noodles and bonding like a proper father and child should at least every third weekend.

Have you seen this Dad?

This type of action-man dad likes to bond with his children, whether it's a footie game, rugby, paintballing, cars or poetry. OK, maybe not poetry.

Never-reads-the-bloody-manual Dad

Nothing frustrates a dad more than going shopping and buying a new gizmo or electrical 'toy' then having to read a manual just so he can simply operate the stupid thing. Imagine the frustration! Dads don't want to read the manual. They want to ignore the manual! They want to buy it, unbox it, plug it in and play it. That's it. They don't want to read how it actually works, the warnings, the health and safety and all that nonsense about X goes into Y,

C1 goes into D67 and so on. They want to work all that stuff out for themselves, to hell with the instructions!

Dads who never read the manual lack patience and are by nature incredibly stubborn – but then aren't all dads? Most dads like to be proper men, and proper men don't want to be told how to do things and have to read instructions – they want to dive head first into it and work it out the wrong way round – that way if they bugger it up, they can blame it on *not* reading the manual, like proper men, and *not* because they didn't know what they were doing.

Pushy-for-their-own-good Dad

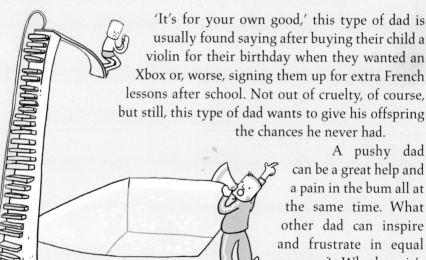

'It's for your own good,' this type of dad is usually found saying after buying their child a violin for their birthday when they wanted an Xbox or, worse, signing them up for extra French lessons after school. Not out of cruelty, of course, but still, this type of dad wants to give his offspring the chances he never had.

A pushy dad can be a great help and a pain in the bum all at the same time. What other dad can inspire and frustrate in equal measure? Whether it's encouraging their children to achieve what they consider the impossible (e.g. the slightest amount of revision for GCSE Maths) right through to encouraging them to jump off the highest springboard at the local swimming pool because 'It'll do wonders for their confidence' you mumble to mum, who is scared stiff of seeing her little baby go bouncing off up into the ceiling.

A pushy for your own good dad just wants his children to achieve the best in life and the only way they will do so, he believes, is with a little 'pro-active encouragement'. Dad's words, not mine.

'Listen to your Mother' Dad

One of my favourite types of dad. But not because they are lazy, indifferent and stupid. No, these are one of the best types of dad because they are the ones that are scared of mum. They are the dads who operate in the background of the family decision-making, happy in the knowledge that if mum is making all the plans and taking all the responsibility then nothing can go wrong. In the house, they know mum's opinion matters the most and what mum says goes. Dad is merely the back-up guy, the yes man to mum when she has to put her foot down. If mum says something, the kids believe her. If dad says something the kids are suspicious and have to go double check with mum.

A 'listen to your mother' dad knows that mum holds all the cards, she wears the trousers and it is her word that is gospel not his. Most kids know this as well, which is why most dads are left out of the loop on most things – only being informed of family plans and schedules at the last minute. Dad doesn't need to know. Why? Because he has to do them anyway. Mum's orders. As mum used to say in our house – 'If dad doesn't like it, T.O.U.G.H!'

Have you seen this Dad?

You very rarely hear a dad have an opinion on important family decisions. You are more likely to hear this type of dad say 'Your mother should know!' or 'Whatever *you* think is best' if ever asked a question!

Cool Dad

This is the cool dad. The modern dad, the liberal dad, the dad that understands that modern life and parenting isn't the same as it was back in his day. This is the dad that is 'down with the kids' despite not really knowing what that actually means.

Cool Dad knows that things have changed since he was a kid and he knows that being a dad isn't about being a 'buzzkill' who always says no, it's about being a cool 'rent' who would do anything to be considered trendy, even though he knows the word trendy is no longer trendy.

This type of dad wears the latest fashions, he owns designer brands, he goes to the gym, he downloads the current hot bands from the internet (legally, of course), drags mum to the cinema to see the latest 'flick', he keeps up to date with iPhones and Blackberry (he owns both, just in case) and is the type of dad who spends more time on the Nintendo Wii than the children. Though this dad is also aware that he doesn't want to look like he's trying *too* hard, because, a cool dad knows that would be so seriously uncool.

Useless-in-the-kitchen Dad

Dads who work stressful, on-the-go, 80hr-a-week jobs don't have time, or the inclination, to read cookery books to find out what flavours go together or how to cook things properly – they don't even know how to turn the dishwasher on. That's mum's territory, after all. And, dads will argue, mum is such a great cook, why would he need to learn?

Now, not cooking for mum (or the family) is fine – mums and children appreciate how hard dads work during the week so not being able to cook a magnificent roast dinner is acceptable – but mums and kids must draw the line at not knowing how to operate the toaster. If the children can do it, dad should at least try.

At work, dad is a hard-nosed businessman with the power of ten men. At home, in the kitchen, he's confused by cereal. Where is it? Where does it go? What's this little clip thing?

Mum pities him because he's so useless. He can't use the hobs, he can't use the grill, he can't even work out the symbols on the oven to cook some oven chips.

So what does he do?

Turns on the BBQ!

Reads-all-the-time Dad

Be it daily newspaper subscriptions, the weekend supplements, online or books, the dad that likes to read all the time, likes to read *all* the time. It doesn't matter if he's on the beach, in the car, on a train, on the toilet or in the shower, this type of dad likes to keep ahead of his reading schedule and he likes to know what's going on in the world. This type of dad won't just read any sort of rubbish, oh no! He'll have a bookcase full of books he hasn't read yet so that once he finishes one book he can jump straight into another – whether it's the new Richard Dawkins, Stephen Hawking or Barack Obama biography, this type of dad will have plenty to read. For the next ten years! There will also be three whole bookcases of books that he bought twenty years ago that still haven't been read, taking up space in mum's poor space-deprived living room.

Have you seen this Dad?

You can always tell a dad who likes to read all the time. Instead of the usual toilet books and magazines most people have – for quick glancing through while you're on the throne – this type of dad will have a little bookcase next to the loo, full of epic novels, you know, just in case he ends up in there for longer than expected.

Famous Dads Through the Ages: A Timeline!

God
(13 billion-ish years ago)
Dad of the world (if, indeed,
he is a man) and baby Jesus.

Dad's Army (1968)
The most inept bunch of
dads in Walmington-on-Sea

Father Time (well old)
The personification of time. Another
beardy bloke with time on his hands.

Father Christmas
(4th century-ish)
The most famous dad in the
world (for one day a year at
least). Massive beard. Jolly
fellow. You know the one.

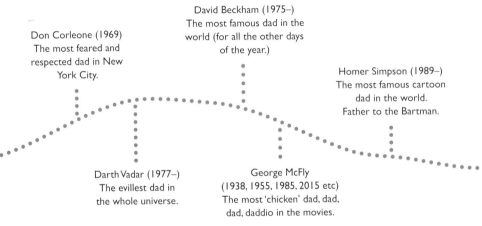

Don Corleone (1969)
The most feared and respected dad in New York City.

David Beckham (1975–)
The most famous dad in the world (for all the other days of the year.)

Homer Simpson (1989–)
The most famous cartoon dad in the world. Father to the Bartman.

Darth Vadar (1977–)
The evillest dad in the whole universe.

George McFly
(1938, 1955, 1985, 2015 etc)
The most 'chicken' dad, dad, dad, daddio in the movies.

Always-affectionate-with-Mum Dad

This type of dad is, of course, a particular favourite of mums across the country. However, the kids would prefer it if dad kept his PDA's (Public Displays of Affection) to himself – for fear of embarrassment, yes, but also because 'old' people still showing their love for one another is 'well gross'.

Well, this dad doesn't care if it's 'gross', 'sick' or 'wicked', a publicly affectionate dad doesn't care where he is or who is watching, he loves mum and wants to give her a smooch, cuddle or even a cheeky fondle of the bottom to show her how much he loves her and how much he can't keep his hands off her. The kids may groan, but that's fine, when do they not? An affectionate dad isn't afraid to show mum, and his kids, and indeed the whole world, how he feels out in public and mum certainly doesn't complain – though she may get a touch giggly if dad's hands get a bit busy when in the car park of B&Q.

This type of dad is like a flirty teenager, always trying to get in a cheeky squeeze and snuggle wherever he can. Not that dad would call it a 'snuggle' – that's a mum word. This type of dad would call it something completely different.

Bob-Dylan Dad

Dads, across the world, are so renowned for their bad taste in music it can actually define them. It doesn't even depend upon when they were born, most dads will have some utterly terrible music in their collection (which is now gathering dust in the loft as mum doesn't want it in the house). Usually with dads, and it doesn't matter when they were born, Bob Dylan will be God. They will own all of his records (the good, the bad and the *Under the Red Sky*) and while they would admit that 'he has had his down moments' will not hear a bad word said against him!

This kind of Dad's music collection will, hardly ever have anything modern in it, which means that he would have been listening to the same ten albums, by the same five artists, for the past four decades – this will, of course, mean that dads reference point for what makes good and bad music is pretty slim. This dad will dismiss new artists when compared to the 'legendary, proper stars' of the 1960s and 70s despite many of them now being old codgers and still churning out the same songs they were signing when dad was a kid.

Good-laugh Dad

Dads like to embarrass their kids. It's pretty much the main reason why they wanted to become a dad, in fact. Why do you think they dress kids up in silly clothes and hats when they are babies and then take photos? It's so that they can embarrass the same child 18 years later in front of his new girlfriend or school mates.

The Good-laugh Dad, however, takes it to a whole new level. He is the type of dad that is constantly good fun to be around – telling jokes, tickling, running around like a lunatic, will never say no to a piggy-back ride and is always ready to drop everything he is doing and go play a bit of footie in the garden.

A Good-laugh Dad is forever getting in trouble with mum, whether it's stopping off for a quick ice cream in the park (before dinnertime) or letting the kids stay up late to watch a scary movie because 'it's a classic of modern cinema'.

The Good-laugh dad is always on hand to cheer his kids up after a hard day at school, by making sure they always go to bed with a smile on their face and knowing that daddy loves them very much.

Have you seen this Dad?

Most dads are Good-laugh Dads when the kids are young. Though, sadly, most turn into Grumpy-old-man dads after the kids have grown up and moved away because they have no one to entertain and make laugh any more. Except mum, but she doesn't count.

Beer Dad

One of the most common types of dad there is. The Beer Dad can be spotted most days either gently supping a pint of home-made ale (which looks a lot like a dirty puddle) at the local pub or finishing off a few 'tins' of lager at the neighbour's house while watching the golf. A Beer Dad has his favourite type of beer but isn't fussy when it comes to making a choice – as long as it's tasty and wet and quenches every bone in his body after a hard day's work, he won't mind.

Beer Dad makes his own beer in the shed, going to great lengths and consideration to look after it, nurture it (even singing to it) so that it tastes like sweet golden honey nectar.

Of course, it goes without saying, the Beer Dad has a beer belly. This can vary in size depending on how well the belly is looked after – whether it is fed daily with beer or just two to three times a week. A big beer belly needs feeding at least once a day, whereas a medium-size belly probably only needs beer two or three times a week.

A proper beer dad hasn't seen his toes since 1987 but can still wiggle them, so at least he knows they are still there.

Hard-working Dad

While it's fun to make fun of dad, poking him in his beer belly and using his house as a hotel, it's easy to forget that dads actually have a day job that they work hard at to provide for the family. Most kids think that dads magic money from thin air and have a whole forest of little money trees in the back garden along with mum's vegetables. The truth is they don't! Dads work hard and make sacrifices so that it only seems that way.

A dad who works hard is a stressed dad. This type of dad will come home after a long, tiring day and, quite frankly, not be in the mood to listen to their daughter try and play the violin or help his son revise for a maths test. But hard working dads do … no matter how busy their day has been, they will always find the time to help out at home. Perhaps even stopping by the kitchen first to give mum a quick kiss and moan about his day while she makes a cup of tea with a biscuit.

This type of dad knows that he is a good dad and tries his best to be there as often as he can and, come the end of the night, when the kids are tucked in, and mum is on the sofa waiting for him to unwind, dads can finally relax. It might be 11.05pm, but this is dad's time. And a good time for a glass of wine…

Doctor Dad

Dads are proud creatures. They want to be there for their children whenever something goes right, wrong, good, bad or just not quite as hoped. Dads hate being useless when it comes to helping out their children and they hate knowing that they can't help. Though they don't mind being useless at helping mum with the house chores do they?

Anyway, when a son cuts his knee or when a young daughter is poorly with a sniffle, dad is always first to the rescue with the medicine, the first aid kit and comforting words of 'Don't worry! Dad's here!!!'

All dads are doctor dads, really. Some dad's are actual doctors, but for those who aren't, this type of dad does his best to evaluate the situation, sum up what's wrong, diagnose as best as he can and then dole out the medicine, treatment or kisses to the hurting area that he feels is necessary. Whether it's a hanky, a cold flannel, a hug, a mug of Lemsip or the worst attempt at bandaging a cut leg you've ever seen, doctor dads are always the best emergency response unit. Unless, of course, it's 'just a scratch' in which case doctor dads have no sympathy whatsoever!

Have you seen this Dad?

Doctor dads are great when it comes to speedy ambulance-style driving to the hospital. They are less great when having to sit in a doctor's waiting room one minute longer than they have to, grumbling incoherently about the NHS under their breath.

Wine-connoisseur Dad

From Ancelotta to Zinfandel and everything in between, a wine connoisseur dad is a man who enjoys 'fruity little numbers'. Whether it's a 'nosy', 'zesty' or 'heady' Barbarossa, an intense 'cab sav' or even a 'zingy' Grignolino, dad knows them all – and he even knows all the right words to describe the correct wines so as not to make a fool of himself in restaurants!

This type of dad will own a drip dickey to avoid any wastage (especially of the Chateau Haut Brion Pessac-Lognan, 1982) and will have his own little wine cellar in the garage where he keeps wine in 'drink by' date order – maybe even labelling 'DON'T TOUCH!'

on the more expensive bottles to keep mum away from using it as cooking wine. Dad still hasn't forgiven her for using a bottle of 2003 Saumur-Champigny, Cuvée Prestige (a Loire Pinot!!) in last Tuesday's Bolognese sauce!

In pubs and restaurants, a wine connoisseur dad knows the correct way to swill and taste the wine, and while this may seem like the most embarrassing and pompous public act to perform in front of the family, dad must be totally sure that the wine isn't corked. The smelling, swilling, sucking through teeth and spitting may sound like a visit from a rather rude plumber, but it's actually dad pretending he knows what he is doing in a rather flagrant display of connosieur-ness as he nods to the waiter his satisfaction!

Camera-always-at-the-ready Dad

Golden rule number one about dads: if a dad is nearby, there is a strong chance that a camera is not far behind – lurking, ready, waiting to be used to take the same photo over and over again until he has got the same shot 1,000 times. Dad won't be happy until he's got the perfect shot, and kids will be expected to pose there until he gets it.

Dads love taking photos of their family. They may claim to be 'making memories last forever', but even dads know that that's a lie. Dads just enjoy taking pictures so they can show relatives and friends what a beautiful family they have and show off all the fancy places they've been on the family newsletter every Christmas.

In restaurants or theme parks, this type of dad will ask a waiter/passer-by to get a shot of the family. 'Actually, take two,' dad will say and, upon being given back the camera and checking out the shot, he'll ask for one more 'just for luck' much to the iritation of the press-ganged photgrapher and the dismay of mum and the kids, who have already been grinning inanely for five minutes and fear lockjaw is setting in.' Quit your complaining,' dad will reply!

Do-It-Yourself Dad

The DIY dad. Probably the most famous, or infamous, type of dad in the world, depending, obviously, on how good his DIY skills are. Some dads happily admit they are rubbish and call in the plumber to fix the leak without even trying to fix it for themselves. Other dads like to put on the wellies and overalls and dive straight in without a single clue as to what they are doing.

A DIY dad owns every tool for every job that exists under the roof. From spanners to spare pipes, hacksaws to colour-coded gaffer tape, a DIY dad has it all – a one-man proud sponsor of Black & Decker. Though DIY dads have been known to get a little out of their depth and bite off more than they can chew, a DIY dad will often only admit this just before the house collapses after he has knocked out a load-bearing joist span. Whatever that is.

A DIY dad is a dad that refuses to call a professional in until the 11th hour, by which time a £500 job has spiralled into a £3000 job because dad has made it a lot worse.

Have you seen this Dad?

One of the noises a DIY dad hates most is the sound of a plumber sucking air through his teeth and observing that a small downstairs toilet leak (which he could fix with a bandage) will cost £300 (excluding labour and parts).

Amuse-yourself Dad

Sometimes even the best dad in the world needs a break from being a dad. It's hard work, you know! (No matter what mum might say).

Maybe it's been a difficult day, or week at work, or maybe there is something interesting that dad wants to read or watch (*The Times, The Wire* respectively) – it doesn't matter – sometimes  this dad just likes a good old cup of tea, or a beer, and a sit down to rest his weary legs and have a moment or two to himself. But just because dad is entertaining himself, doesn't mean the kids aren't bothering him to come play or nag him about fixing one of their toys. They may want some quality time with daddy, to use him as a punching bag, wrestle with him, or ask him about their UCAS application form. Most of the time dad will be up for this, but in those rare, moments when this dad just wants to be left alone, all he can offer to his children to shut up and be quiet and 'amuse yourselves', is money. Cold hard cash. This peace offering, quite literally, is a rare gift from dad, who usually hates handing money over so easily to his children. But in his hour (maybe an hour and a half) of need, this offering can appease children, give dad a bit of a break, and means he can regroup later on fighting fit.

Hates-to-admit-he's lost Dad

Men hate admitting they are lost. Dads doubly so, especially when in the car with the whole family and they have been driving around in circles for the past 45 minutes. 'I'm not lost!' dad will claim repeatedly, feeling the kids' eyes burning into the back of his head.

This type of dad stubbornly refuses to use any navigational tool because, to them, its help, and everyone knows how dads don't like help when it comes to getting from A to B. Dads like to use their primeval man instinct, their gut feeling, to get them there instead. Of course, their gut feeling hasn't been mapped by the Ordnance Survey.

On the way to a dinner party, mum will offer knowingly, 'Shall we take the TomTom or the map ... just in case?'. Dad will be dismissive: 'We don't need to ... I remember where I'm going, trust me!'.

Two and a half hours later...

What should have been an easy, half-hour trip to a well-signposted surburban area has turned into an epic odyssey into the heart of the countryside with dad screaming, 'I'M NOT LOST ... IT'S JUST THAT NOTHING LOOKS FAMILIAR!'.

On arrival at their destination, mum will take great pleasure in telling everyone that the reason they are late is not because they 'forgot the map' but because 'my husband is an idiot'.

Rubbish-with-telly Dad

There are some things dads aren't very good at. One of them is lifting the toilet seat up. The other is watching bad television. Very, very rarely will a dad spend his time watching telly with the family who are watching repeats, soaps, children's TV, reality TV or gameshows. He would much rather spend time on his own in the garden, garage or study. While mum and the kids could quite happily watch *X Factor* until the cows come

home, dad, after five minutes of trying, has given up, slated it as 'utter tripe' and stormed out the living room.

This type of dad can be known to be quite vocal about how there is 'nowt on telly these days', sometimes effing and blinding at the idiots on gameshows ('It's A! It's A! You ******* *****!') or celebrity ice dancers in jungles making fools of themselves ('Prats!').

Have you seen this Dad?

This type of dad has been known to throw objects at the TV in protest at the complete rubbish mum sometimes forces him to sit through in order to have some 'family time'.

'When I were a lad' Dad

Some dads, those with good memories anyway, can remember what life was like back when they were a kid, how different it was, and what such exciting times they were before iPhones, TVs and PlayStations came along and distracted everyone from the green rolling hills and cobbled streets of quaint under-populated towns.

They were the 'good old days' this nostalgic dad would say. As if the differences weren't obvious enough between the eras, this type of dad likes to make it abundantly apparent to his own children every five minutes, by saying things like 'It weren't like that when I were a lad!' or 'You kids don't know you're born!' and 'Consider yourself lucky you're not eating gruel for dinner' as if it was Victorian England all of a sudden.

The 'When I were a lad' dad thinks the kids of today are spoilt rotten compared to how it was for him when he was growing up, when all they had for dinner was potatoes and, well, more potatoes and they had to entertain themselves by skimming stones, poking ants nest with sticks and building tree houses – none of this shooting each other with 'plastic toy Uzi's'. When he were a lad he had to use his finger etc etc and so on…zzzzzzzzz

Sober-on-Friday-night Dad

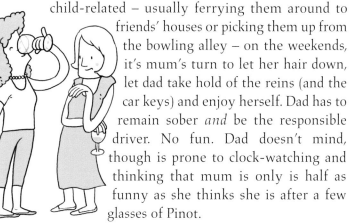

While dad has the weekdays to have a few drinks after work to relax and unwind, letting mum take care of business in the evenings with anything child-related – usually ferrying them around to friends' houses or picking them up from the bowling alley – on the weekends, it's mum's turn to let her hair down, let dad take hold of the reins (and the car keys) and enjoy herself. Dad has to remain sober *and* be the responsible driver. No fun. Dad doesn't mind, though is prone to clock-watching and thinking that mum is only is half as funny as she thinks she is after a few glasses of Pinot.

This type of dad can also be found at home, and as sober as a judge , on a Friday night – on mum's orders – just in case one of their teenage children is out for the night and doesn't come back as per the agreed curfew, and dad needs to be sent out looking for them.

Have you seen this Dad?

This is the reason why dads like to drink in afternoons on weekends. It's so they can go for a nap, sleep it off, and be ready for the evening should they be required by mum later on. Well, this and the fact that dads like drinking on weekend afternoons.

Obviously-dressed-by-mum Dad

There are two types of dads when it comes to clothing and fashion. The first one is the trendy dad who likes to look 'snazzy' and 'cool' and buy the latest all-weather jacket, fancy black leather coat and struts around in Italian loafers looking like an M4-corridor version of George Clooney. The other type of dad is, well, it's the exact opposite of that.

The obviously-dressed-by-mum dad is the type of dad who gave up on fashion and even buying his own clothes a long, *long* time ago. He now relies solely on mum to purchase all his clothing, even his shoes. Now, of course, mum has been buying knickers and socks for the whole family since the first child was born (it's just easier to buy a job lot), but now, due to dad's complete lack of style and indifference to the changing fashion trends, she feels compelled to go out and by all of dad's wardrobe too.

There will be hits and misses, the odd expensive bit of Ralph Lauren ('This Ralph fella must be cold?' dad will joke, 'I've got all his clothes!') and the odd bargain-bin treasure from a charity shop. All of it dad will wear, without care, just as long as it fits and he doesn't look too daft. In fact, he rather enjoys being dressed by mum as, after all these years, she knows his style (or lack thereof) better than anyone, and wouldn't dare to be seen with him if he looked like a vagabond.

Traveller Dad

Most dads like to travel, go on family holidays abroad, take lots of pictures and then come back absolutely knackered and say things like 'I think we need another holiday to get over that one!' or 'Right, that's that done for another year!'

But the traveller Dad – he's a different species altogether. This type of dad lives for family holidays. He spends the whole year planning it to perfection, saving up for it, packing for it – there's even a bag in the spare room collecting maps, discounts and camera batteries, six months in advance!

He's the type of maniacal dad who wakes the kids up three hours earlier than they need to be to get them all excited, jumping up on their bed, eager-eyed and giddy. He also makes sure they are at the airport five hours in advance just in case the 'plane leaves early'.

Whereas most family holidays are children-orientated places like Epcot, Universal Studios and Disneyland traveller dad has planned a two-week road trip through all the EU countries, starting alphabetically with Antartica and ending up in Warsaw. Or a trip up the Amazon. Or a wild dog sled race through Antartica. Traveller dad won't be happy until all the family have passports that look beaten up and stamped to death and have clocked up 4 million air miles with British Airways.

Upon arriving home, while the rest of the family go to bed, jetlagged and exhausted, dad pulls out the atlas and thinks 'Right-i-o, where to next then?!'

Taxi dad

When a child is born, dads are over the moon. They are speechless, tearful and full of incomprehendable emotions. They are delighted to have helped create this beautiful baby with the woman they love. They know that, from that moment on, they will do anything for this person, love it unconditionally, care for it, protect it, sacrifice everything they have so that it has the best life he can provide for it.

What doesn't strike a dad's mind at that precise moment, that beautiful tear-jerking moment, is that he will spend the next 18 years (and more) of his own life, not only being a father, a dad and protectee of this child, he will also become … a taxi driver.

A taxi driver who doesn't get paid.

And a taxi driver who can't charge inflated prices after 10pm.

Oh, and also a taxi driver who is pulled out of bed to go and pick up their teenage daughter after a late-night house party, or to drive the twins back and forth to pre-school swimming or to chauffeur his son (and his friends) to the local football club for training two times a week.

None of this crosses a man's mind before he becomes a father, and it comes as a bit of surprise, years later, when this type of dad realises he has spent more time ferrying people around in the car than he has in his own bed since 1982.

Takeaway Dad

Picture the scene.

Mum's away for the night at her sister's. Dad has no plans. The kitchen looks like a very complicated place. Dad wouldn't know where to begin. The kids are whingeing for some food. Dad would quite like a nice night in on the sofa in front of the telly watching something he wants to watch for a change. What do you think he would do?

Let me give you a clue, it begins with 0-800-BRING PIZZA!

For those types of dad that are whizzes in the kitchen, takeaway dad may appear rather obselete.

But for the majority of dads who can't boil an egg, let alone make an omelette, then this probably sounds like the beginnings of a dad's perfect night in.

With mum gone, dad will revert back to being a teenager, and the kids will run riot, but as long as they stay off his radar and stay out of trouble, then takeaway dad won't care. Besides, he's got a motorcycle to take apart on the kitchen table and drink beer in his pants.

Have you seen this Dad?

This type of dad orders takeaway not because he enjoys the taste or think it's better than mum's cooking. No, it's because there is no washing up involved after. The boxes go straight in the recycling bin. Job done!